What's Underneath

Poems

Jane Sasser

Iris Press Chapbook Series
Oak Ridge, Tennessee

ISBN: 978-1-60454-510-4

Cover Photo: Jason Leung

Book Design: Robert B. Cumming, Jr.

Iris Publishing Group, Inc
www.irisbooks.com

Acknowledgments

Thanks to the publications where these poems have previously appeared:

Appalachian Heritage: "Chiaroscuro," "Every Leaving"
Avocet: "The Origin of All Poems"
In God's Hand: "Fig Preserves"
Mildred Haun Review: "The Ghosts of My Parents Diagnose My Dog"
Number One: "Apology," "Ars Canis," "Character Test," "Foundations,"
    and "Missing"
Pine Mountain Sand & Gravel: "My Mother, My Country, and My Dog
    Explain Heaven"
POEM: "Marking Time," "Memento Vivere"
Rockvale Review: "What's Underneath"
Santa Fe Literary Review: "Ode to the Level"
Still: The Journal: "Love Poem"

Contents

What's Underneath

By the time backhoe bites
pavement, he is there:
a skinny kid, maybe nine

years old, his bike propped
against utility pole, and
he is standing in the street,

watching. From my window
I see the twitch of his shoulder
blades, his worn white sneakers

edging inches toward the hole, and
I see how the workers let him
join their circle, remembering,

perhaps, how it was to be a boy,
endless lessons of summer
mornings, whole world waiting

outside the door. All morning
he stands witness, taut as wire,
learning what we'd all like to know:

what lies under the surface
of things, that thinnest veneer
over which our lives drive.

I. What Grounds Us

The Origin of All Poems

Stop this day and night with me and you shall possess the origin of all poems.
—Walt Whitman

It starts with an image bubbling
on my tongue and then
a whole world opens,
a door through which words trickle
or if I'm lucky, flood
so I have to grab the bucket
to catch the flow. Or perhaps
it's a window I unlatch to hear
frogs sing on the first warm night
or wind as it tangles the chimes,
no tune ever the same as the last.
Sometimes it's a phrase someone says,
maybe even misheard, words opening
memory or possibility like a bud unfurling
to summer sun. Or it's the things
I don't know at all, things
I can never know but can't
let go, and here, on this page,
I grapple or spin until my mind
can see. It's because I want both
the worlds and the words
of Emily Dickinson, enigmas
almost lost but compelling
as pollen to bees.

Love Poem

Because you rise at four A.M.
to let out the dog who has to pee.

Because you scatter drawings of objects
you plan to invent, sketched on backs

of torn envelopes. Because, like your mother,
you crave chocolate like cocaine.

Because, though I am the teacher,
you assign random grades: a B for that movie,

C+ for this soup. Because when
you assess me, you grade

on a curve.

Fig Preserves

1.

First, find the plant,
after two years' search,
green lobed leaves nodding
in the pot by the nursery door.

2.

Next, dig the hole by
a south-facing wall,
fill with good black dirt,
water well, and wait.

3.

Pray for sunny days,
warm and thick, spelled
by summer rains, months
where branches stretch
toward a white-hot sky.

4.

Wait two years, through winters
that could freeze it black,
back to determined roots.
If luck holds, maybe
they won't.

5.

At last, figs appear,
like commas swollen
into rounds, green
into gold, then freckled,
plum, and plump.

6.

Slice lemons into wheels,
acid to cut honeyed pulp,
cook syrup rich and brown,
warm and thick as
those summer days.

7.

Pour liquid jewels into jars,
sealed with pings for
January mornings, pleasure
as old as the fruit and leaves
from the tree of knowledge.

Infinite

On December 24, 1968, Apollo 8
—the first manned mission to the Moon—
went into lunar orbit; that evening,
the astronauts broadcast from space.

In the beginning there was the truck,
my father, me, and Christmas Eve.
Darkness moved on the face of the sky,

but there was light—the stars—
and on the radio, the crackle
of space, of astronaut's voice

and Genesis 1, as we huddled
between cow smells and God
and knew it was endless, and good.

Foundations

for my mother

Belly to belly with earth,
she lies beneath the house,
below galaxies of web,
each one a Milky Way draped
from the oak beams' dark sky.
Safe from summer's sun,
from brothers flaunting worms
and jokes meant to break
the walls of her quiet,
she nestles and reads,
a secret she shouldn't know
but does. She steals
her sisters' books,
stashes them in a stack
behind chimney stones.
They won't complain.
In this house, filled
to the brim with squabbling
life, everything gets lost, even
the youngest girl. Now
she rolls onto her back,
probes with her toes
the underside of floors
she's walked for seven years,
waiting for her chance
to go to school,
to probe undersides
of worlds she's never glimpsed,
winking like stars she sees
from the porch steps at dusk.

Ode to the Level

that you use to measure
the angles of the parts
of this house: ceiling grid,
door, windows, cabinets, trim—
all of it settled and sagged
from seventy-odd years
of sweet living—your parents' lives,
and yours, wearing edges
into soft memories, touch
of fingers, soles, scarred table
where they ate and passed worlds
through lips warmed by coffee,
hands curled around cups,
so like your hands as you hold
the old level, eye its gold bubble,
and straighten this framework,
true, level, and steady
like dreams of their thousands
of days.

Déjà vu

I circle back to my old neighborhood,
back, an old friend says, to the right side
of the tracks, back to working class soil

where I struck my deep roots. I settle,
like the wren in my hanging plant,
where I'm sure I belong, something

in our genes convinced this place
calls our first names. Scruffy lawns
and overhead wires mean only

we can relax, standards are slack.
Wrenlike, I shape this small nest,
woven of arching oaks, birdsong,

sky blue days. She lays her brief egg,
and I dream of sweetness to come,
unstructured bliss before time

winds down.

Memento Vivere

Beautiful as they are, please do not feed the chickens
—sign in Haworth Graveyard

The chickens in the graveyard do not care
if Branwell brooded and wallowed
in opium and his father's neglect.

And if Charlotte and Emily penned
masterpieces in tiny script, sitting
at the same table where they ate

their meals, while their reverend father
may or may not have shot pistols
from the porch, the chickens are content

to scratch the moss, waddle, and preen
without concern. If Anne coughed
and understood she was the one

we would all forget, the chickens
do not discriminate, thinking only
of grubs and whatever wrongful treats

some Bronte lover throws their way.
But when storms slant across the moors,
grasses blowing and singing in the wind,

the chickens exult—their crowing ensures
there will be unquiet slumber for the sleepers
in this quiet earth.

Elegy for a Country Childhood

The crisp sound of a hoe in dirt,
pointed blade severing morning glories
from cornstalks, tomato plants,
dew heavy as rain, sticking blades
of grass to bare feet. Sun burning
a hole through morning's mist.
The odors of manure, of hay,
of gardenia blooms. Acres of pasture
and red clay, plowed and planted:
soybeans, corn, sugar cane. Always
a faithful dog, matted, free,
rich in the stench of canine joy.
The sounds of cows: lowing, cropping grass,
their snorts and warm breath. The slam
of the screen door, crackle of ice
broken free from aluminum trays,
glasses of tea on the warm brick steps.
The house across the road, weathered gray,
returning to earth, its broom straw yard.
Baptism in a neighbor's pond, rising
muddy and cleared of sin
on a sticky summer afternoon.
Slow trickle of years, punctuated
by Sunday pound cakes, seasons flashing by
like Kodak slides projected
on the chartreuse dining room wall.

Every Leaving

is a death,
even the ones I think
I desired, the packing
of wool sweaters

for morning walks
through falling leaves
to college classes,
or boxes numbered and taped

for the move from
a long-loved home,
or holiday guests
who crowded our rooms,

towels and plates piled
in the wake of flurried goodbyes,
whose absence now
is a haunting lack.

In January dark
so cold it could break
like actual ice
I will drop you

for your flight,
driving to work
and trying to think
of my students, who

will shuffle to class
in their wool sweaters,
dimly aware of their own
looming leavings, and you

will be somewhere overhead,
soaring through dawn,
back to the life
you have chosen as yours.

II. What Haunts Us

Chiaroscuro

The shadow you cast is a darkness
in which we all flounder, wish
we knew more than the outline
of your life, black and white photos
we shuffle through, glimpses
that leave us to guess: you,
in a white shirt and cotton ducks
rolled up, crossing Rocky River
to church in the johnboat you called
the bateau. From the overhanging branches
at the shore, your paddle raised
in morning light, a snake sifts
from a tree, circles your arm,
sloughs to the water below.
Or you, home from the war,
crutches in hand, missing a step
on concrete stairs, how you spilled
through bright air, made the choice
to swing your mending legs to spare
your heavy head, how when you hit
and rolled, you felt them snap again.
Or you, driving a bus through the dark,
that time—so tired—you followed white line
up an exit and sat and wondered
how you'd come to this place, and how
you drove that bus down and back into night.

Morning Routine

What time do you want to get up?
my mother asked each time,
though she was in her eighties now,
and I a wife, mother, teacher, long

capable of rising on my own.
I should have said *seven o'clock.*
I should have let her believe
she would remember that I

was there, sleeping in the guest
room, let her think she would
rise early and make pancakes,
we would plan a day of shopping,

going out to eat, as though
she wouldn't get up in the night,
eat ice cream and dream
of home, in the morning

sleeping like the dead as I
poured cereal in our bowls.

Ordinary Wood

In the Hong Kong gift shop,
I turned the box in my hands,
its whorls of deep grain and red hue

unknown to me. *What wood is this?*
I asked, and the clerk shrugged.
Ordinary wood. Maybe the words

did not translate, as when my friends
said *green vegetable* when I asked
about a dish. Language at best

encircles a thing, makes clumsy
attempts to capture its soul,
as we orbit our sun. In the long years

of my mother's passing,
as memories dimmed and tangled
like threads, grief circled, silent,

hard as heartwood of oak.
Sometimes a loss is a shriek, a tearing
of skin. But sometimes instead

it's a smooth, stiff plank, familiar
to us but impermeable. It's the slump
of a tree, the splinters of hope,

sawdust of one's heart.

Hauntings

My mother threatened to haunt me.
Get in line, I wanted to say,
behind the endless dreams
of classes I neglected to attend,

exams I forgot to take, school buses
I missed while I couldn't decide
what dress I should wear, or worse,
places I went having failed

to wear clothes, lovers who jilted me,
cities I wandered, lost,
so many ways to go wrong, all
probed as I slept by worries

that refused to rest. So haunt me,
I should have said. You'll be
one kind face in a chaos
of loss.

Apology

for Jim

I'm sorry. I was so young
then, and didn't know
that your unsmiling face
in the class photograph,

the glint of light on glasses
unfashionably uncool,
hinted what horror you hid
at home. I'm sorry I didn't

try to understand, afraid
I'd catch cooties somehow
by speaking to a boy,
one who didn't like dodgeball

at recess, stood under
the oak. I'm sorry school
was just another prison,
and there are no second chances

to make that change. I wish
I had spoken, summoned
strength to claim my own voice.
I wish I had known you

when you needed that most.

Outcast

Two nights before school starts,
I lie awake, suddenly knowing
in my cells I will never belong
to the farm again, that chapter

of my life closed without
my comprehension until now,
and I am haunted by memory
of standing where the path curved

between arcs of summer's gifts,
corn, tomatoes, squash on my right,
rows of butterbeans and zinnias
nodding on my left, all hung

in morning glories and early dew.
I cannot fall to sleep because
I can't remember her final garden,
when it was plowed, how many years

before her death, cannot remember if,
after my father died in May,
she went on picking beans,
jarring tomatoes, freezing corn,

lining pantry shelves with food
we'd find and toss twenty years
from then. I don't want
these memories, not now, when

I should be dreaming about
being lost at school, so much easier
than this orphanhood, this exile
it will be my lot to bear.

How It Ends

We're all curious about what might hurt us
—Federico García Lorca

I imagined you dead.
When you were late
coming home from work
or the airport or store,
I would think, what if you
had fallen from the air
and were smeared on some field,
or you were immolated
on the road in a fiery crash,
or you were caught in a shootout
between rival gangs,
or fell over on the sidewalk
of a massive heart attack?
There would be a little crying,
and then life insurance to pay
off your debts, and then
I could box your hoarded books,
magazines, stacks of VHS tapes,
my landscape scraped clean
and light for my new
ordered life.

III.   What Loves Us

Ars Canis

The euphoria of dogs in the evening,
their people coming home—bliss of muscles
flexed, racing, and oh! the smells

of squirrels, leaves, muddy red clay—and
kibble in bowls, and ear rubs,
at last circling, sinking into beds.

In wee hours, shuffle of paws
outside closed bedrooms, hearts' need
to count and account for all

the loved pack.

Sorry. The Dog Ate Your Homework.

All those papers, discharging funk
of so many homes: cigarette smoke,
sautéed garlic, beef stew,
takeout tacos, Tide, Bounty,
moth balls, air freshener,
Abercrombie & Fitch, dogs
of all breeds, sweat, smeared oil
of your hands, a hundred
of them, spread like seasoning
across these white sheets,
like meat sandwiched in canvas
bag, too much to resist,
the tear of them in euphoric teeth
like the pleasure of a kill.

The Ghosts of My Parents Diagnose My Dog

Reckon she's got the scours,
my father says, which rhymes
with *fires*, and is no doubt
how it feels to her. He knows
how it can fell a cow, healthy,
then suddenly gaunt with loss.
My mother favors tapeworm,
reminds us of that cousin
who ate whole fried chickens,
mounds of creamed potatoes,
plate upon plate of pie
and cake, and still her calves
were like sticks, her face
like a pointed shrew's.
My mother holds out her hands,
measures how long it was,
says, *Afterwards, she got so fat.*

Marking Time

Waking from my afternoon nap,
I lie on the sofa watching green leaves
flutter against a sky so blue, September
clearly on them both, even though
I know if I opened the door summer heat
would hang as heavy as it has
for months. And I think how earth turns,
hurrying us on through our days and lives,
how yesterday I sat in a waiting room,
where someone had hung a calendar,
each day marked off with a giant X.
Although it was just past noon,
that day was marked, its sentence
set, and I wondered, who hates
her time so much, that showing up
means a battle won? *You're wishing
your life away*, my mother would say
when I yearned for some future date.
In September, perhaps, of my own life
now, I think how Shakespeare thought
of time: like a year, like a day, like
a fire burning out, and in her bed,
my dog—crippled with age and pain,
her bones stark curves under sagging
skin—sighs and turns, and we both go
on, wishing for more warm days.

Character Test

It was only a dog, he declares,
dismissing her life to a list
of minor things lost or misplaced:
cat-eye marbles, gym sock,
an earring's mate, the eighth
stainless spoon. And in black ink
I write his name on my list
of people I don't trust, fold
it shut, flick my wrist and
bend to toss it, captainless,
a boat on the water's flush.

Missing

After she died, the rain ceased,
like pathetic fallacy gone wrong,
and why not, since everything else
already had. Our three hearts

parched as surely to powdered waste
as sere leaves on great oaks, as grass
like splinters under stunned steps.
Autumn slumped into dry despair,

sky gray with smoke of acres burning
grief. When at last cool drops fell,
we lay stiff in our beds, ears cocked,
insides scraped clean as desert bones.

My Mother, My Country, and My Dog Explain Heaven

It's really a wonderful place, my mother says.
That designer who claimed she'd run away
with my husband if I put a chenille spread
on my bed, that man at the hospital who announced
that my baby was a girl before I could,
that state representative who accused me
of not being a Christian before he was arrested
in a prostitute sting, none of them
are here.

Hey, girl! my country yells from the window
of its new double cab pickup truck.
It's all great now! All the white men
have jobs, and we love this huge
new wall. Best of all, we can say whatever
the hell we want. So get your butt back
into the kitchen and fix me a steak.

Mom! Mom! my dog barks, wagging her tail.
I can run free as wind, and my hind legs
don't drag. Every day smells like
chicken stew, and there are fields
of lavender where I can rub
my face, and I can lie forever
in this warm, sweet light.

Assessment

> Macbeth: *What is the night?*
> Lady Macbeth: *Almost at odds with morning, which is which.*

Winter morning so early
it is almost at odds with night
as to which is which, I wake

slowly to the sound of whimpers
down the hall, the younger dog
lonesome for his pack, and I lie

warm in the fortress of our bed,
weighing the costs: counseling
for the dog versus the chance

of Alzheimer's for me,
sleep-deprived, though there is also
the chance you could wake, too—

answer his calls—but not this time.
The clock you wish I would just
throw out glows the hour: right after four,

and besides his cries, there's the sound
of breathing, soft and deep, and whisper
of heat in the floor vents. I ponder

what I will do in the extra hours
before dawn, then scoop my glasses
from the stand, open the door, and

journey toward his morning joy.

Jane Sasser was born and raised on a farm in Fairview, NC. She grew up in a family of storytellers and began writing her own stories at the age of six. Her poetry has appeared in *JAMA, North American Review, The Sun,* and other publications. She has published two poetry chapbooks, *Recollecting the Snow* and *Itinerant*. A retired high school English teacher, she lives in Oak Ridge, TN, with her husband and retired greyhounds.